Connolly

by Iain Gray

Lang**Syne**

PUBLISHING

WRITING *to* REMEMBER

LangSyne

PUBLISHING

WRITING *to* REMEMBER

E-mail: info@lang-syne.co.uk

Distributed in the Republic of Ireland by Portfolio Group,
Kilbarrack Ind. Est. Kilbarrack, Dublin 5.
T:00353(01) 839 4918 F:00353(01) 839 5826
sales@portfoliogroup.ie
www.portfoliogroup.ie

Design by Dorothy Meikle   Printed by Ricoh Print Scotland

ISBN 978-1-85217-247-3

Connolly

MOTTO:
In God is all.

CREST:
A hand grasping a chaplet (signifying joy).

NAME variations include:
Ó Conghalaigh *(Gaelic)*
Ó Coinheallaigh *(Gaelic)*
Ó Conghaile *(Gaelic)*
O'Conolly
O'Connolly
Connally
Connelly
Connelay
Coneley
Conolly

Chapter one:
Origins of Irish surnames

According to an old saying, there are two types of Irish – those who actually are Irish and those who wish they were.

This sentiment is only one example of the allure that the high romance and drama of the proud nation's history holds for thousands of people scattered across the world today.

It's a sad fact, however, that the vast majority of Irish surnames are found far beyond Irish shores, rather than on the Emerald Isle itself.

The population stood at around eight million souls in 1841, but today it stands at fewer than six million.

This is mainly a tragic consequence of the potato famine, also known as the Great Hunger, which devastated Ireland between 1845 and 1849.

The Irish peasantry had become almost wholly reliant for basic sustenance on the potato, first introduced from the Americas in the seventeenth century.

When the crop was hit by a blight, at least 800,000 people starved to death while an estimated two million others were forced to seek a new life far from their native shores – particularly in America, Canada, and Australia.

The effects of the potato blight continued until about 1851, by which time a firm pattern of emigration had become established.

Ireland's loss, however, was to the gain of the countries in which the immigrants settled, contributing enormously, as their descendants do today, to the well being of the nations in which their forefathers settled.

But those who were forced through dire circumstance to establish a new life in foreign parts never forgot their roots, or the proud heritage and traditions of the land that gave them birth.

Nor do their descendants.

It is a heritage that is inextricably bound up in the colourful variety of Irish names themselves – and the origin and history of these names forms an integral part of the vibrant drama that is the nation's history, one of both glorious fortune and tragic misfortune.

This history is well documented, and one of the most important and fascinating of the earliest sources are *The Annals of the Four Masters*, compiled between 1632 and 1636 by four friars at the Franciscan Monastery in County Donegal.

Compiled from earlier sources, and purporting to go back to the Biblical Deluge, much of the material takes in the mythological origins and history of Ireland and the Irish.

This includes tales of successive waves of invaders and settlers such as the Fomorians, the Partholonians, the Nemedians, the Fir Bolgs, the Tuatha De Danann, and the Laigain.

Of particular interest are the *Milesian Genealogies*,

because the majority of Irish clans today claim a descent from either Heremon, Ir, or Heber – three of the sons of Milesius, a king of what is now modern day Spain.

These sons invaded Ireland in the second millennium B.C, apparently in fulfilment of a mysterious prophecy received by their father.

This Milesian lineage is said to have ruled Ireland for nearly 3,000 years, until the island came under the sway of England's King Henry II in 1171 following what is known as the Cambro-Norman invasion.

This is an important date not only in Irish history in general, but for the effect the invasion subsequently had for Irish surnames.

'Cambro' comes from the Welsh, and 'Cambro-Norman' describes those Welsh knights of Norman origin who invaded Ireland.

But they were invaders who stayed, inter-marrying with the native Irish population and founding their own proud dynasties that bore Cambro-Norman names such as Archer, Barbour, Brannagh, Fitzgerald, Fitzgibbon, Fleming, Joyce, Plunkett, and Walsh – to name only a few.

These 'Cambro-Norman' surnames that still flourish throughout the world today form one of the three main categories in which Irish names can be placed – those of Gaelic-Irish, Cambro-Norman, and Anglo-Irish.

Previous to the Cambro-Norman invasion of the twelfth century, and throughout the earlier invasions and settlement of those wild bands of sea rovers known as the Vikings in the eighth and ninth centuries, the population of the island was relatively small, and it was normal for a person to be identified through the use of only a forename.

But as population gradually increased and there were many more people with the same forename, surnames were adopted to distinguish one person, or one community, from another.

Individuals identified themselves with their own particular tribe, or 'tuath', and this tribe – that also became known as a clann, or clan – took its name from some distinguished ancestor who had founded the clan.

The Gaelic-Irish form of the name Kelly, for example, is Ó Ceallaigh, or O'Kelly, indicating descent from an original 'Ceallaigh', with the 'O' denoting 'grandson of.' The name was later anglicised to Kelly.

The prefix 'Mac' or 'Mc', meanwhile, as with the clans of the Scottish Highlands, denotes 'son of.'

Although the Irish clans had much in common with their Scottish counterparts, one important difference lies in what are known as 'septs', or branches, of the clan.

Septs of Scottish clans were groups who often bore an entirely different name from the clan name but were under the clan's protection.

In Ireland, septs were groups that shared the same name and who could be found scattered throughout the four provinces of Ulster, Leinster, Munster, and Connacht.

The 'golden age' of the Gaelic-Irish clans, infused as their veins were with the blood of Celts, pre-dates the Viking invasions of the eighth and ninth centuries and the Norman invasion of the twelfth century, and the sacred heart of the country was the Hill of Tara, near the River Boyne, in County Meath.

Known in Gaelic as 'Teamhar na Rí', or Hill of Kings, it was the royal seat of the 'Ard Rí Éireann', or High King of Ireland, to whom the petty kings, or chieftains, from the island's provinces were ultimately subordinate.

It was on the Hill of Tara, beside a stone pillar known as the Irish 'Lia Fáil', or Stone of Destiny, that the High Kings were inaugurated and, according to legend, this stone would emit a piercing screech that could be heard all over Ireland when touched by the hand of the rightful king.

The Hill of Tara is today one of the island's main tourist attractions.

Opposition to English rule over Ireland, established in the wake of the Cambro-Norman invasion, broke out frequently and the harsh solution adopted by the powerful forces of the Crown was to forcibly evict the native Irish from their lands.

These lands were then granted to Protestant colonists, or 'planters', from Britain.

Many of these colonists, ironically, came from Scotland and were the descendants of the original 'Scotti', or 'Scots', who gave their name to Scotland after migrating there in the fifth century A.D., from the north of Ireland.

Colonisation entailed harsh penal laws being imposed on the majority of the native Irish population, stripping them practically of all of their rights.

The Crown's main bastion in Ireland was Dublin and its environs, known as the Pale, and it was the dispossessed peasantry who lived outside this Pale, desperately striving to eke out a meagre living.

It was this that gave rise to the modern-day expression of someone or something being 'beyond the pale'.

Attempts were made to stamp out all aspects of the ancient Gaelic-Irish culture, to the extent that even to bear a Gaelic-Irish name was to invite discrimination.

This is why many Gaelic-Irish names were anglicised with, for example, and noted above, Ó Ceallaigh, or O'Kelly, being anglicised to Kelly.

Succeeding centuries have seen strong revivals of Gaelic-Irish consciousness, however, and this has led to many families reverting back to the original form of their name, while the language itself is frequently found on the fluent tongues of an estimated 90,000 to 145,000 of the island's population.

Ireland's turbulent history of religious and political strife is one that lasted well into the twentieth century, a landmark century that saw the partition of the island into the twenty-six counties of the independent Republic of

reland, or Eire, and the six counties of Northern Ireland, or
Ulster.

Dublin, originally founded by Vikings, is now a vibrant
and truly cosmopolitan city while the proud city of Belfast
is one of the jewels in the crown of Ulster.

It was Saint Patrick who first brought the light of
Christianity to Ireland in the fifth century A.D.

Interpretations of this Christian message have varied
over the centuries, often leading to bitter sectarian conflict –
but the many intricately sculpted Celtic Crosses found all
over the island are symbolic of a unity that crosses the
sectarian divide.

It is an image that fuses the 'old gods' of the Celts with
Christianity.

All the signs from the early years of this new
millennium indicate that sectarian strife may soon become a
thing of the past – with the Irish and their many kinsfolk
across the world, be they Protestant or Catholic, finding
common purpose in the rich tapestry of their shared
heritage.

Chapter two:

Fierce as wolves

Bearers of the Connolly name, in all its variety of spellings, are to be found all over the present day Republic and in Northern Ireland – but the ancient province of Connacht was their original homeland.

The clan gradually split up into a number of septs, such as the Connollys of Monaghan and the Connollys of Ulster, but what they all had in common was that their name derived from Ó Conghalaigh, or Ó Coinheallaigh, indicating descent from Conghal, or Congal, with 'Conghal' denoting 'fierce as a wolf', or 'valorous.'

It would prove to be a very apt description for this clan that for centuries was at the forefront of the struggle against foreign invasion and in the battle for their country's freedom and independence.

It was the Connollys of Monaghan who became recognised as 'Chiefs of the Name', in honour of the high distinction they held as one of the members of the Four Tribes of Tara, along with the O'Hares, the O'Regans, and the O'Kellys.

Tara, in present day Co. Meath, was the sacred site of the enthronement of the Ard Rí, or High King, of Ireland.

The four tribes were part of the great clan confederation that formed the southern Hy Niall, or Uí Neill, that traced a descent from Fiacha, a son of the legendary Niall

Noíghiallach, better known to posterity as the great warrior king Niall of the Nine Hostages.

The dramatic life and times of this ancestor of the Connollys are steeped in stirring Celtic myth and legend.

The youngest son of Eochaidh Mugmedon, king of the province of Connacht, his mother died in childbirth and he was brought up by his evil stepmother Mongfhinn who, for reasons best known to herself, was determined that he should die.

She accordingly abandoned him naked on the Hill of Tara, but he was found by a bard who took him back to his father.

One legend is that Mongfhinn sent Niall and his four brothers – Brian, Fiachra, Ailill, and Fergus – to a renowned prophet who was also a blacksmith to determine which of them would succeed their father as Ard Rí.

The blacksmith, known as Sitchin, set the lads a task by deliberately setting fire to his forge.

Niall's brothers ran in and came out carrying the spearheads, fuel, hammers, and barrels of beer that they had rescued, but Niall staggered out clutching the heavy anvil so vital to the blacksmith's trade.

By this deed, Sitchin prophesied that Niall would be the one who would take on the glorious mantle of kingship.

Another prophetic incident occurred one day while Niall and his brothers were engaged in the hunt.

Thirsty from their efforts they encountered an ugly old woman who offered them water – but only in return for a kiss.

Three of the lads, no doubt repelled by her green teeth

and scaly skin, refused. Fiachra pecked her lightly on the cheek and, by this act, she prophesied that he would one day reign at Tara – but only briefly.

The bold Niall, however, kissed her fully on the lips. The hag then demanded that he should now have full sexual intercourse with her and, undaunted, he did so.

Through this action she was suddenly transformed into a stunningly beautiful young woman known as Flaithius, or Royalty, who predicted that he would become the greatest High King of Ireland.

His stepmother Mongfhinn later tried to poison him, but accidentally took the deadly potion herself and died. This legend relates to what was known as the Festival of Mongfhinn, or Feis na Samhan (the Fest of Samhain) because it was on the evening of October 31, on Samhain's Eve, that the poisoning incident is said to have taken place.

It was believed for centuries in Ireland that, on Samhain Eve, Mongfhinn's warped and wicked spirit would roam the land in hungry search of children's souls.

The Festival, or Feast, of Samhain, is today better known as Halloween.

Niall became Ard Rí in 379 A.D. and embarked on the series of military campaigns and other daring adventures that would subsequently earn him the title of Niall of the Nine Hostages.

The nine countries and territories into which he raided and took hostages for ransom were the Irish provinces of Munster, Leinster, Connacht, and Ulster, Britain, and the territories of the Saxons, Morini, Picts, and Dalriads.

Niall's most famous hostage was a young lad known as Succat, son of Calpernius, a Romano-Briton who lived in the area of present day Milford Haven, on the Welsh coast.

Later known as Patricius, or Patrick, he became renowned as Ireland's patron saint, St. Patrick, responsible for bringing the light of Christianity to the island in the early years of the fifth century A.D.

Raiding in Gaul, in the area of Boulogne-sur-mer in present day France, Niall was ambushed and killed by one of his treacherous subjects in 405 A.D.

It was through their descent from Niall's son, Fiacha, that the southern Hy Niall clans such as the Connollys of Monaghan were also known as Cenel Fhiachaigh, or Fiachach.

The 'Congal' from whom the Connellys took their name was a chieftain in the tenth century A.D. of the southern Hy Niall.

Adding further lustre to the Connolly pedigree is that the Connollys of Monaghan also traced a descent from Mahon, a brother of the great warrior king Brian Boru and progenitor of the proud clan McMahon.

It was Brian Boru who, on Good Friday 1014, defeated a mighty Viking army at the battle of Clontarf, about four miles north of Dublin.

Late tenth and early eleventh century Ireland was the scene of vicious inter-clan rivalry as successive clan chiefs fought for supremacy over their rivals.

It was this disunity that worked to the advantage of the

Norman invaders of the late twelfth century and the Viking invaders of previous centuries.

The period 795 A.D. to 1014 A.D. is known to Irish history as The Viking Tyranny, and it was largely through the inspired leadership of Brian Boru that Viking power was diminished, although not completely eliminated.

He was able to achieve this by managing to rally a number of other chieftains to his cause – although by no means all.

Boru, also known as Brian Bóruma and the ancestor of the distinguished O'Brien clan, was a son of Cennetig, king of Dál Cais, in the northern reaches of the province of Munster.

With his battle-hardened warriors known as the Dalcassian knights at his side, Boru had by 1002 A.D. achieved the prize of the High Kingship of Ireland – but there were still rival chieftains, and not least the Vikings, to deal with.

These Vikings, known as Ostmen, had occupied and fortified Dublin in the mid-ninth century and had other important trading settlements on other parts of the island.

Resenting Boru's High Kingship, a number of chieftains, particularly those of the province of Leinster, found common cause with the Ostmen, and the two sides met in final and bloody confrontation at Clontarf.

Boru was victorious, but the annals speak of great slaughter on the day, with the dead piled high on the field of battle.

Among the many dead were his three sons, while he was killed in his tent by a party of fleeing Vikings – but not before felling most of them with his great two-handed sword.

Chapter three:

In freedom's name

Less than sixty years after the death of Brian Boru, Ireland was in the grip of another wave of foreign invasion – this time in the form of Norman knights who had crossed the Bristol Channel from Wales.

By 1171 they had taken Dublin and other strategically important territories.

England's King Henry II, who had given tacit acceptance to the invasion, now began to take cold feet over the venture, realising that he may have created a rival in the form of a separate Norman kingdom in Ireland.

Accordingly, he landed on the island, near Waterford, at the head of a large army in October of 1171 with the aim of curbing the power of his Norman barons.

Protracted war between the king and his barons was averted, however, when they submitted to the royal will, promising homage and allegiance in return for holding the territories they had conquered in the king's name.

Henry also received the submission and homage of many of the Irish chieftains, tired as they were with internecine warfare and also perhaps realising that as long as they were rivals and not united they were no match for the powerful forces the English Crown could muster.

English dominion over Ireland was ratified through the

Treaty of Windsor of 1175, under the terms of which some native Irish clan chieftains were allowed to rule territory unoccupied by the Normans in the role of vassal.

Over the following centuries the English grip on Ireland was consolidated as further waves of Anglo-Norman settlers settled on the island, at the expense of many native Irish such as the Connollys of Monaghan who were steadily pushed and dispersed from their lands.

A simmering cauldron of discontent and resentment had been created – one that would boil over periodically in subsequent centuries with particularly dire consequences for the Connollys and other Irish clans.

The cauldron boiled over in 1641 in the form of a rebellion by the Catholic landowners against the English Crown's policy of settling, or 'planting' loyal Protestants on Irish land.

This policy had started during the reign from 1491 to 1547 of Henry VIII, whose Reformation effectively outlawed the established Roman Catholic faith throughout his dominions.

This settlement of loyal Protestants in Ireland continued throughout the subsequent reigns of Elizabeth I, James I (James VI of Scotland), and Charles I.

In the insurrection that exploded in 1641, at least 2,000 Protestant settlers were massacred at the hands of Catholic landowners and their native Irish peasantry, while thousands more were stripped of their belongings and driven from their lands to seek refuge where they could.

Terrible as the atrocities were against the Protestant settlers, subsequent accounts became greatly exaggerated, serving to fuel a burning desire on the part of Protestants for revenge against the rebels.

Tragically for Ireland, this revenge became directed not only against the rebels, but native Irish Catholics such as the Connollys in general.

The English Civil War intervened to prevent immediate action against the rebels, but following the execution of Charles I in 1649 and the consolidation of the power of England's fanatically Protestant Oliver Cromwell, the time was ripe for revenge.

The Lord Protector, as he was named, descended on Ireland at the head of a 20,000-strong army that landed at Ringford, near Dublin, in August 1649.

The consequences of this Cromwellian conquest still resonate throughout the island today.

Cromwell had three main aims: to quash all forms of rebellion, to 'remove' all Catholic landowners who had taken part in the rebellion, and to convert the native Irish to the Protestant faith.

An early warning of the terrors that were in store for the native Catholic Irish came when the northeastern town of Drogheda was stormed and taken in September and between 2,000 and 4,000 of its inhabitants killed, including priests who were summarily put to the sword.

Cromwell soon held Ireland in a grip of iron, allowing

him to implement what amounted to a policy of ethnic cleansing.

His troopers were given free rein to hunt down and kill priests, while Catholic estates such as those of the Connollys were confiscated.

Resistance to a series of harsh penal laws enacted against the native Irish over subsequent centuries only fuelled the flames of rebellion, most notably in an abortive rebellion in 1798.

Rebellion in a most spectacular form occurred more than 100 years later in the form of the 1916 Easter Rising in Dublin – a Rising in which arguably one of the most famous bearers of the name of Connolly played a prominent and ultimately tragic role.

This was the socialist and republican Séamus Ó Conghaile, better known to posterity as James Connolly, the son of immigrants to Scotland from County Monaghan and who was born in Edinburgh in 1868.

By the age of 14 he had enlisted in the British Army, spending the bulk of his seven-year service in Ireland and witnessing what he perceived as the particularly harsh and brutal treatment of the native Irish at the hands of the British authorities.

He returned to Scotland following his discharge from the army, and it was here that he first became involved in the socialist movement, serving as secretary to the Scottish Socialist Federation.

By 1896 he was back in Ireland, serving in Dublin as secretary to the Dublin Socialist Society, forerunner of the Irish Socialist Republican Party, later spending some time in the United States as a member of the Socialist Party of America.

Returning to Ireland he was a co-founder in 1913 of the Irish Citizen Army (I.C.A.), and later the founder of the Irish Labour Party.

As the bitter struggle for Irish independence from British rule intensified, Connolly's I.C.A. joined forces with the Irish Republican Brotherhood (I.R.B.) to mount the Easter Rising of 1916, known in Irish as Éiri Amach na Cásca, following a proclamation of independence signed by Connolly and six others.

With Connolly as Commandant of the Dublin Brigade, the aim was to wrest independence from Britain by force of arms and, accordingly, on April 24, Easter Monday, the combined republican forces of the I.C.A. and the I.R.B. seized strategic locations throughout Dublin, including the General Post Office.

Other Risings were timed to take place simultaneously throughout the counties of Galway, Wexford, and Louth.

With a force of less than 5,000 republicans matched against no less than 16,000 well armed and trained troops and 1,000 armed police, the Rising was doomed to failure – coming to a bloody and exhausted conclusion on April 30th after its leaders were forced into reluctant surrender.

More than 1,200 republicans, troops, police, and civilians had been killed, but further deaths followed as the sixteen leaders of the Rising, including James Connolly, were executed by the British Crown in Dublin's Kilmainham Jail.

Connolly had been severely wounded in the fighting and, despite being an already dying man, he was executed on May 12.

There was international outrage when it was learned that, too weak to stand, he had been taken to the execution yard and tied to a chair, and then shot by firing squad.

A statue of James Connolly now stands in Dublin.

His son, Roddy Connolly, was aged 15 when he served under his father during the Rising in Dublin.

He later became a member of the Irish Labour Party and was elected to the Irish Parliament as member for Louth in 1943 and serving on the Irish Senate between 1975 and 1977.

He died in 1980.

Chapter four:

On the world stage

Far from the field of conflict generations of Connollys, in all the variety of spellings of the name, have achieved fame in a range of pursuits

Fondly known as 'The Big Yin', **Billy Connolly** is the highly versatile Scottish comedian, musician, actor, and presenter with an international reputation who was born in the Anderston district of Glasgow in 1942.

Leaving school at the age of 15, in common with many working class Glasgow lads of his generation, he entered the clamour and sweat of the shipyards, serving a five-year apprenticeship as a welder.

His taste for adventure found an outlet in the Parachute Regiment of the Territorial Army, while in 1965 he was in Nigeria employed in building oilrigs.

Returning to his native land his ambitions became focussed on music, as a banjo-playing member of the folk-pop duo The Humblebums, before he turned his talents to stand-up comedy.

Best-selling albums of his comedy routines followed, in addition to sell-out performances on stages throughout the world.

He has also appeared in a number of television situation comedies in addition to acclaimed performances in a number of films, including the 1997 *Mrs Brown*, the 1999 *The Boondock Saints*, the 2003 *Samurai*, and the 2006 *Fido*.

He is the recipient of numerous awards, including an honorary Doctor of Letters from Glasgow University, a CBE in the Queen's Birthday Honours List, a BAFTA Lifetime Achievement Award, and an honorary doctorate from the Royal Scottish Academy of Music and Drama, in Glasgow.

A best selling biography of Connolly, *Billy*, written by his second wife, the actress Pamela Stephenson, was published in 2003.

Born in New York City in 1943, **Kevin Connolly** is the actor and film director who directed the 2007 *Gardener of Eden*, while in the world of music **Tyler Connolly**, born in 1975 in North Delta, British Columbia, is the vocalist and lead guitarist of the Canadian rock band Theory of a Deadman.

In the world of the printed word **John Connolly**, born in 1968 in Dublin, is the best-selling Irish crime writer who is best known for his series of novels starring American private detective Charlie Parker.

Published in 1999, his first novel, *Every Dead Thing*, was nominated for the Bram Stoker Award for Best First Novel, and won the 2000 Shamus Award for Best Private Eye Novel.

He is also a regular contributor to the *Irish Times* newspaper.

Born in 1950, **Joseph Connolly** is the British writer whose novel *Summer Things* was adapted for the film screen in France in 2002 as *Embrassez qui vous voudrez*, while his *Jack the Lad and Bloody Mary* was published in 2007.

A former prosecutor for the state of Montana, **C.P. Connolly**, born in 1863 and who died in 1935, was the American investigative journalist whose work was for many years featured in the mass-circulation *Collier's Weekly*.

Born in Coventry in 1903, **Cyril Connolly** was the English literary critic and intellectual who was also a contemporary and friend of the author George Orwell.

Co-editor of the literary magazine *Horizon* from 1939 to 1950 Connolly, who died in 1974, was also for a time the chief book reviewer for the *Sunday Times*. His autobiography *Enemies of Promise* was published in 1938.

In the world of politics **Harold Connolly**, born in 1901 in Sydney, Nova Scotia, and who died in 1980, was the politician, journalist, and newspaper editor who served as Canada's Liberal Premier in 1954.

His newspaper career began with the *Halifax Chronicle*, and he later served as editor of the *Daily Star*. Retiring from provincial politics in 1955, he was subsequently elevated to the Canadian Senate.

Born in 1750 in Slane, Co. Meath, and later immigrating to America, **Bishop John Connolly** became the second bishop of the Roman Catholic diocese of New York, 41 years after being ordained a priest.

John Connolly, born in 1860 in Victoria, was a celebrated Australian gold prospector and mine owner who owned several mines in New South Wales.

It was Connolly who discovered a platinum field at Fitfield and, in 1890, the Nannine gold field near Cossack, in Western Australia. Before his death in 1928 he had also prospected for gold in both New Zealand and New Guinea.

Connollys have also excelled in the highly competitive world of sport, not least the American athlete **James B. Connolly**, born in 1868 in South Boston, Massachusetts, and who became the first modern Olympic champion.

Born into a poor background and one of twelve children, Connolly had to leave school at an early age, finding work as a clerk with an insurance company and later enlisting with the United States Army Corps of Engineers.

By dint of hard study he was accepted in 1895 to study Classics at Harvard University – but withdrew as a student in 1896 when the university refused to grant him leave of absence to attend the Olympic Games that year in Athens, Greece.

The International Olympic Committee had been created in 1894, and the 1896 games were the first modern edition of the Olympics.

The triple jump was the first final on opening day – an

vent that Connolly won, making him the first Olympic champion since 385 A.D.

He also took a silver medal at the 1900 Paris Olympics.

Turning his talents to journalism, Connolly reported for the *Boston Globe* newspaper on the Spanish-American War and later became an expert in the field of maritime writing.

In 1920 he was a crewmember of the schooner Esperanto, winner of the first International Fishing Schooner Championship Races, held off Nova Scotia.

Author of 25 novels and more than 200 short stories, the multi-talented **James B. Connolly** died in 1957.

On the football pitch **Matthew Connolly**, born in 1987, is the English footballer who, at the time of writing, is defender for top club Arsenal, while **David Connolly**, born in 1977 is the Irish professional footballer who, at the time of writing, plays for English club Sunderland.

Between 1997 and 2001, when he was signed to Dutch club Feyenoord, the striker was the highest paid player in Dutch football.

Born in 1963 **Chris Connolly** is the former Australian rules footballer who played more than 80 games with the Melbourne Football Club. At the time of writing he is coach of Freemantle Football Club.

In the world of baseball **Tom Connolly**, born in 1870 in Manchester, England, was a celebrated Major League umpire.

Aged 15 when his family immigrated to America, the young Connolly became captivated by the game of baseball and immersed himself in the complexities of the baseball rulebook.

As an umpire, he officiated in the National League from 1898 to 1900, followed by service in the American League from 1901 to 1931.

Recognised as having helped to establish the high standards of umpiring, he was elected to the Baseball Hall of Fame in 1953. He died in 1961.

Born in 1981 in Baldwinsville, New York, **Tim Connolly** is the American ice hockey player who has played for the Erie Otters of the Ontario Hockey League, while on the cricket pitch **Alan Connolly**, born in 1939 in Skipton Victoria, is the former Australian medium paced bowler who played in 29 Tests.

Arguably the most famous Connolly to have excelled in the world of sport was the American tennis player **Maureen Connolly** – better and more fondly known as 'Little Mo.'

Born in San Diego, California in 1934 her childhood passion was horse riding but, with her family unable to pay the cost of lessons, she turned her attention to tennis.

It proved to be an inspired choice. At the age of 14 she won no less than 56 straight matches, while a year later she became the youngest ever to win the U.S. National Championships for girls aged 18 and under.

In 1953 Little Mo entered the Grand Slam tournaments the Australian, French, and U.S. Championships and Wimbledon) and won, making her the first woman to win the Grand Slam.

In all, she won the Australian Championships once, the French Championships twice, the U.S. Championships five times, and Wimbledon on three straight occasions – 1952, 1953, and 1954.

Tragedy struck in July of 1954, however, shortly after winning her last Wimbledon title, when her right leg was crushed in a road accident while horse riding.

Her distinguished playing career was over at the age of only 19 but, undaunted, she became a popular tennis correspondent for newspapers while, along with her husband Norman Brinker, she set up the Maureen Connolly Brinker Foundation to promote junior tennis.

The tennis legend was inducted into the International Tennis Hall of Fame in 1969, the year of her death, and into the International Women's Sports Hall of Fame in 1987.

Key dates in Ireland's history from the first settlers to the formation of the Irish Republic:

circa 7000 B.C.	Arrival and settlement of Stone Age people.
circa 3000 B.C.	Arrival of settlers of New Stone Age period.
circa 600 B.C.	First arrival of the Celts.
200 A.D.	Establishment of Hill of Tara, Co. Meath, as seat of the High Kings.
circa 432 A.D.	Christian mission of St. Patrick.
800-920 A.D.	Invasion and subsequent settlement of Vikings.
1002 A.D.	Brian Boru recognised as High King.
1014	Brian Boru killed at battle of Clontarf.
1169-1170	Cambro-Norman invasion of the island.
1171	Henry II claims Ireland for the English Crown.
1366	Statutes of Kilkenny ban marriage between native Irish and English.
1529-1536	England's Henry VIII embarks on religious Reformation.
1536	Earl of Kildare rebels against the Crown.
1541	Henry VIII declared King of Ireland.
1558	Accession to English throne of Elizabeth I
1565	Battle of Affane.
1569-1573	First Desmond Rebellion.
1579-1583	Second Desmond Rebellion.
1594-1603	Nine Years War.
1606	Plantation' of Scottish and English settlers

1607	Flight of the Earls.
1632-1636	Annals of the Four Masters compiled.
1641	Rebellion over policy of plantation and other grievances.
1649	Beginning of Cromwellian conquest.
1688	Flight into exile in France of Catholic Stuart monarch James II as Protestant Prince William of Orange invited to take throne of England along with his wife, Mary.
1689	William and Mary enthroned as joint monarchs; siege of Derry.
1690	Jacobite forces of James defeated by William at battle of the Boyne (July) and Dublin taken.
1691	Athlone taken by William; Jacobite defeats follow at Aughrim, Galway, and Limerick; conflict ends with Treaty of Limerick (October) and Irish officers allowed to leave for France.
1695	Penal laws introduced to restrict rights of Catholics; banishment of Catholic clergy.
1704	Laws introduced constricting rights of Catholics in landholding and public office.
1728	Franchise removed from Catholics.
1791	Foundation of United Irishmen republican movement.
1796	French invasion force lands in Bantry Bay.
1798	Defeat of Rising in Wexford and death of United Irishmen leaders Wolfe Tone and Lord Edward Fitzgerald.

1800	Act of Union between England and Ireland.
1803	Dublin Rising under Robert Emmet.
1829	Catholics allowed to sit in Parliament.
1845-1849	The Great Hunger: thousands starve to death as potato crop fails and thousands more emigrate.
1856	Phoenix Society founded.
1858	Irish Republican Brotherhood established.
1873	Foundation of Home Rule League.
1893	Foundation of Gaelic League.
1904	Foundation of Irish Reform Association.
1913	Dublin strikes and lockout.
1916	Easter Rising in Dublin and proclamation of an Irish Republic.
1917	Irish Parliament formed after Sinn Fein election victory.
1919-1921	War between Irish Republican Army and British Army.
1922	Irish Free State founded, while six northern counties remain part of United Kingdom as Northern Ireland, or Ulster; civil war up until 1923 between rival republican groups.
1949	Foundation of Irish Republic after all remaining constitutional links with Britain are severed.